I0439721

OCS Study
MMS 2002-072

Coastal Marine Institute

Effect of the Oil and Gas Industry on Commuting and Migration Patterns in Louisiana: 1960-1990

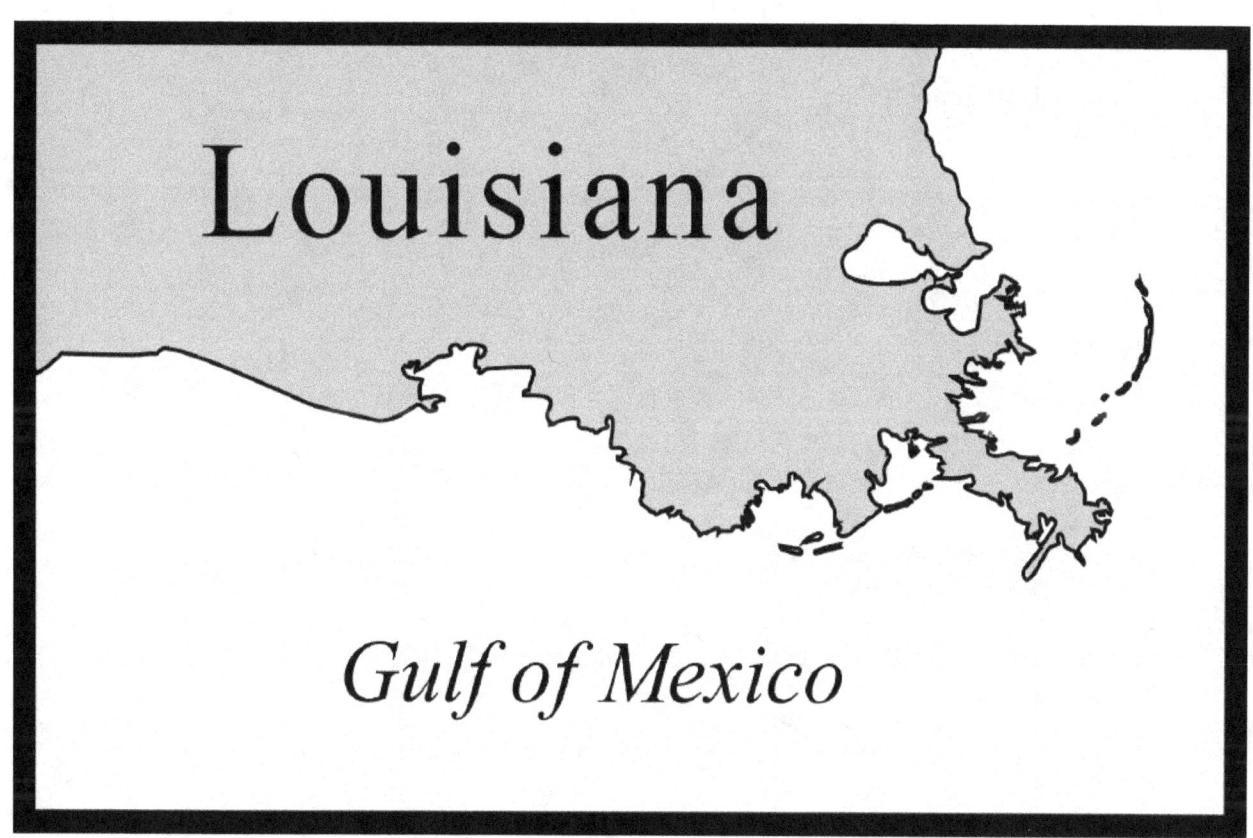

Louisiana

Gulf of Mexico

U.S. Department of the Interior
Minerals Management Service
Gulf of Mexico OCS Region

Cooperative Agreement
Coastal Marine Institute
Louisiana State University

OCS Study
MMS 2002-072

Coastal Marine Institute

Effect of the Oil and Gas Industry on Commuting and Migration Patterns in Louisiana: 1960-1990

Authors

Natusumi Aratame
Joachim Singelmann

December 2002

Prepared under MMS Contract
14-35-0001-30660-19939
by
Departments of Sociology and Rural Sociology
Louisiana State University
Baton Rouge, Louisiana 70803

Published by

U.S. Department of the Interior
Minerals Management Service
Gulf of Mexico OCS Region

Cooperative Agreement
Coastal Marine Institute
Louisiana State University

DISCLAIMER

REPORT AVAILABILITY

CITATION

Table of Contents

List of Figures

List of Tables

1. Overview

The oil and gas industry comprises a very important part in the history and economy of coastal states in the Gulf of Mexico (GOM) region. In Louisiana in particular, where the impact of the oil and gas industry is the greatest, the history of oil and natural gas extraction dates back to the turn of the present century. After the discovery of the Heywood well six miles from Jennings in 1901, oil wells have been drilled in many parts of Louisiana, including Caddo, Webster, Claiborne and Union parishes in the north, La Salle parish in the central part of the state, and in most coastal parishes in the south and in the GOM off the Louisiana coast. The Exxon refinery in Baton Rouge, which is the largest oil refinery in the United States, went on-stream in 1909.

While drilling in Louisiana's coastal marsh areas became an important source of production in the 1920s, the advancement of new technology in the 1940s lead to the drilling in the Outer Continental Shelf (OCS). The first oil well off the Louisiana coast, located 45 miles south of Morgan City, was brought on-line in 1947. The production of oil and gas soared with more discoveries of oil fields in the GOM. Since the 1970s, however, the production gradually declined with the drop in reserves. Most recently, however, a large-scale exploration is under way in the deep water of the GOM. This push further off the Louisiana coast has been made possible by two major developments: first, more accurate 3-D mapping technology that has sharply lowered the number of dry wells, thus reducing the cost of exploration; and second, construction of taller platform structures suitable for deep-water drilling.

1.1. The Oil and Gas Production and Fiscal and Employment Structure in Louisiana

The oil and natural gas industry has been an important source of revenue and employment in Louisiana throughout these periods. The industry contributes a significant proportion in State revenue through the severance tax which, in turn, is used to finance various social and economic activities throughout Louisiana. A significant part of the severance tax (sometimes up to 90 percent) has been used to finance the public school system, with the remaining proportion given back to the parishes. The strong impact of the industry on Louisiana's labor force is reflected in employment changes in the extractive industry that mirror the fluctuation of oil and gas production.

While oil and gas production declined continuously from the 1970s to the early 1990s, the proportion of the severance tax, the number of workers employed in this industry, and the number of wells display more irregular patterns.

The production of oil and gas peaked in 1969-70 and declined consecutively until 1990 due largely to declining reserves. The severance tax, on the other hand, peaked twice (in 1974 and 1981) before it declined to much lower levels in the 1980s. The increase in the severance tax in the 1970s and 1980s resulted from an increase in oil prices that compensated for the decline of production after 1970. The first "oil shock" in 1973-74 and decontrol of oil prices that started after 1979 raised the oil prices dramatically and continuously since 1974, from $3.89 (bbl) in

1

1973 to $31.8 in 1981. Oil prices, however, plunged once again after 1981, which resulted in a declining severance tax.

The number of wells in the GOM region increased rapidly in the 1960s when production was also rising, but they did not drop with the decline of oil/gas production. The number of active wells remained relatively stable after 1984, despite the general downward trend in production.

The number of workers employed by the oil and gas industry does not follow the pattern in production or the number of wells before 1970. The employment peak came in the early 1980s, approximately 10 years after the peak in the production of oil and gas. It is possible that the rising oil prices and declining oil reserves in the late 1970s motivated the industry to bring in more workers in order to find more producing wells. Employment in the oil and gas industry declined substantially as oil prices declined during the 1980s.

To summarize, the impact of the oil and gas industry on revenues and employment is explained by (1) the amount of production and (2) oil prices, with the latter affecting the revenue and employment structure more strongly after 1974 in particular. Until 1973, when oil prices were stable, the amount of oil and gas production, the severance tax, the number of wells and employment only show a weak association. The contribution of the severance tax to state revenue sharply increased to 40 percent in 1974 but declined to 14 percent in 1990, as the price of oil declined. The number of workers employed in this industry essentially followed the movement in the price of oil. Employment reached its peak when the price of oil was highest but declined thereafter.

2. Employment Pattern by Coastal and Non-Coastal Parishes

The employment effect of the oil and gas industry at the parish level differs from the general pattern described above. Some parishes have been more affected by the general fluctuation in the industry than others; the effect may also have changed over time. For example, as the reserve went lower, once booming sites may have curtailed their operation independent of the demand for oil and rising or declining oil prices. As drilling technologies advanced, once inaccessible oil reserves became accessible, benefiting coastal parishes. Below, we will briefly describe the employment pattern over time.

2.1. Coastal and Non-Coastal Parishes: 1960-90 Censuses

Table 1 shows how the total number of workers and the number of workers in the mining industry grew between 1960 and 1990, based on the decennial censuses. We refer here to the mining industry instead of the oil and gas industry, because the breakdown of the mining industry into its component categories before 1980 is not available at the county level.

Before discussing Table 1, we call attention to two properties of the data. First, since the data are collected at the place of residence rather than the place of work, some workers counted in non-coastal areas may be working in coastal areas, and workers enumerated in coastal areas may have jobs in non-coastal areas. Since the differences in data collected at the place of work and

2

place of residence suggest the presence of commuting, the very subject of this research, we will look into this problem more carefully in later sections of this report.

Second, the mining industry includes metal, coal, and nonmetallic mining in addition to oil and gas extraction. However, this aggregation is a less serious problem in Louisiana where more than 95 percent of workers in the mining industry are engaged in oil and gas extraction. For 1980 and 1990, a special tabulation by the Census office with more detailed industrial categories supplements our analysis.

Table 1 indicates that, as was shown in earlier figures, employment in mining steadily increased between 1960 and 1980; it especially increased between 1970-80 when the price of oil rose, and it declined between 1980 and 1990, when the price fell. While both total employment and mining employment rose, the latter grew by a much larger margin between 1970 and 1980. During the period 1980-90, however, the number of mining workers decreased by more than 35 percent on average, while total employment maintained the same level as before.

The differentiation of employment changes in the mining industry by coastal and non-coastal parishes reveals that, somewhat contrary to our expectation, the number of workers in mining doubled in the non-coastal parishes during the period 1970-80 (105 percent), while it increased in coastal parishes by only 46 percent. In the subsequent period, the difference in the rate of decline between two areas is much smaller (-40 and -30 percent, respectively).

The greater increase in mining-related employment in non-coastal areas between 1970 and 1980 is also observed in Table 2, which shows the number of parishes by the extent of oil dependency for the period 1960-90. Between 1970 and 1980, the number of parishes generally increased in those categories that have a greater proportion of mining employment. For example, the number of parishes in the 10 percent and more employment in mining increased from 9 to 13 between 1980 and 1990. Similarly, the number of parishes in the 2.5-5.0 percent category increased from 19 to 26, whereas the number of parishes in the category with the lowest proportion of mining employment (0-2.5 percent) decreased from 27 to 15. The breakdown by coastal and non-coastal parishes shows that the majority of the increase in the categories with a higher proportion of mining employment took place in non-coastal parishes.

There was a change in employment in the mining industry from 1970-1980. Some parishes had growth rates of mining employment higher than the state average (74.6 percent). The category with the highest rates of growth in mining employment is an indicator of the parishes that grew twice as fast as the state average. Except for St. Tammany (which we classify as a coastal parish), all areas shaded darkest are clearly located in non-coastal areas. All coastal areas except Vermillion, on the other hand, showed slower growth than the state average.

The growth of mining employment is a reflection of the economic boom and bust in the respective parishes that affect the industries. The comparison of mining and total employment growth indicates the relative growth of mining is greater in non-coastal parishes than in coastal areas.

# 3.	Commuting

It was noted above that the growth of employment in the mining industry during the period 1960-90 in general, and during the boom years during the 1970s in particular, took place most of all in the non-coastal areas. This fact suggests that commuting and migration may have increased more in non-coastal areas than in coastal areas during the same period, to the extent that the magnitude of commuting and migration often reflects the growth of employment.

In analyzing the effect of employment on commuting and migration, however, it is important to recognize that what appears to be the effect of employment might reflect the effects of respective time periods, locational characteristics, or differences in industrial composition. In this section, we will briefly investigate the commuting pattern related to (1) *period pattern*: the period 1960-1990; (2) *locational characteristics*: coastal and non-coastal areas; and (3) *industrial composition*: the relative share of employment in the mining industry versus all other industries. We expect to find that the volume of commuting in coastal and non-coastal areas is highest in those areas with the largest share of employment in mining. We further expect that commuting plays a larger role in the mining industry in coastal areas as compared to non-coastal areas.

## 3.1.	Commuting Patterns 1960-90

In general, the proportion of commuters among workers in Louisiana has steadily increased during the period 1960-90 as the number of commuters grew faster than that of workers: The number of commuters has increased four-fold during this period (from 104,485 to 412,605 persons), while the number of total workers almost doubled (from 943,217 to 1,630,341) (see Table 3). In terms of growth rates, the number of commuters increased substantially during the periods 1960-1970 (83 percent) and 1970-1980 (99 percent), and they maintained a modest growth between 1980 and 1990 (9 percent). Total employment, in comparison, had the largest increase between 1970 and 1980 and showed practically no growth during the period 1980-90 (Table 4). As a result, the proportion of commuters among total workers increased from 11.1 percent in 1960 to 24 percent in 1980, and it continued to increase to 25 percent despite a decline in the growth rates in commuting during the recent period.

Throughout this period, the eleven coastal parishes in Louisiana consistently received more commuters than the state's 53 non-coastal parishes combined. The proportion of commuters among workers, as a result, has been much higher in coastal areas than in non-coastal areas. In 1960, 16 percent of all workers in coastal areas were commuters, compared to only 7.8 percent in non-coastal areas. By 1990, while the difference between coastal and non-coastal areas slightly narrowed, 32 percent of workers in coastal areas were commuters versus 21 percent in non-coastal areas. The smaller difference between coastal and non-coastal areas in the percentage of commuters resulted mostly from the differential growth in commuting during the period 1970-80; during his period, total and mining-related employment grew more in non-coastal areas than in coastal areas, as noted previously.

In summary, commuting has been an important source of workers in coastal areas during the period 1960-90. Commuting appears to be also sensitive to the growth of the economy as

4

reflected in the growth of employment. The importance of commuting as a source of labor increased during this period, but the gap between the coastal and non-coastal areas somewhat diminished, owing to a greater increase of commuting in non-coastal areas in response to a greater employment growth between 1970 and 1980.

3.2. Commuting Patterns by Industry

The importance of commuting in coastal areas is generally in line with our prediction that commuting is an important source of workers for coastal parishes that relay on (offshore) mining activities. However, the data presented above do not allow us to conclude that the mining industry *per se* attracts more commuters than other industries; it may be other industries that are actually attracting these commuters. Consequently, it is necessary to disaggregate the commuting flows in terms of industry. For 1980 and 1990, the Journey-to-Work data from the 1980 and 1990 Census provide a further breakdown of commuting workers in terms of the major industry categories (one-digit industrial classification).

Tables 5 and 6 show the number and percentage of commuters by industry in coastal and non-coastal areas for 1980 and 1990. The breakdown clearly shows that mining (which combines agricultural services, forestry, fisheries and mining) includes the highest proportion of commuting workers for both periods. In 1980, 39 percent of workers in mining were commuters; only the construction industry had a comparable percentage of commuters in that year. In 1990, the proportion of commuting in mining industry increased to 43 percent. In comparison, workers in trade, public and private services and government employees are more likely to be residents of the area where they work. A further breakdown by coastal and non-coastal areas reveals that for all industry categories, workers in coastal areas are more likely to be commuters than is the case for workers in non-coastal areas. This applies especially to mining: about one-half of mining employment in coastal areas (47 percent in 1980 and 52 percent in 1990) is made up by commuters.

These findings clearly demonstrate that (1) coastal areas depend heavily on commuting workers as a source of employment, and (2) the mining industry especially attracts workers who commute from elsewhere. The assessment of the impact of non-resident workers in coastal areas, however, must include the areas from which workers are recruited; of particular interest here is the distance of commuting as an indication of the geographical spread of the attraction of mining employment in coastal areas.

We therefore carried out an analysis of commuting networks to find out (1) how far the impact of commuting involving coastal areas extends in general and (2) which parishes in particular are involved in commuting networks for sending mining-related workers.

4. Commuting Networks and Commuting Distance

In this section, we present commuting data in several different ways to find out how coastal and non-coastal areas are joined by commuting networks. First, for the period 1960-90, we describe how commuting networks extend from coastal areas compared with non-coastal areas, to be followed by a more detailed description of individual coastal parishes. Since commuting networks might differ by industry, we also investigate the industry differential of commuting for the period 1980-90 (which is the only period for which a breakdown of commuting flows by industry is available).

4.1. Commuting Distance

As shown above, coastal areas, regardless of industry, rely much more on commuting workers than do non-coastal areas. It is possible that a substantial portion of commuters observed in coastal areas originate in a few non-coastal areas that are adjacent to coastal parishes. However, it is more likely that a greater number of non-coastal parishes are involved to meet a demand for commuting workers in coastal areas as the pool of potential workers in adjoining parishes is exhausted. In view of the particular work schedule of OCS activities requiring the presence of workers on the platforms for 1-3 weeks at a stretch (to be followed by at least one week off work), we expect many more workers in coastal areas to originate in distant places than in non-coastal areas, for such a work schedule allows for much longer-distance commuting than would be feasible with a daily 8-5 work schedule.

Table 7 shows the average commuting distance for the period 1960-90 by coastal and non-coastal parishes. Distance is measured from the center of one parish to the other. The data presented in Table 7 demonstrate that coastal parishes recruited workers from slightly more distant parishes in every period than did non-coastal parishes. The difference between coastal and non-coastal areas during this period increased from 3.9 miles in 1960 to 12 miles in 1990. Thus, not only do coastal parishes recruit workers from more distant places than do non-coastal parishes, this difference has increased over time.

The same data are tabulated in terms of a 10-mile radius to investigate the distribution of commuters, which is another important aspect of the spatial dimension of commuting (see Table 8). This table shows the proportion of commuters by 10-mile distance categories for coastal and non-coastal parishes. Since there are no parishes adjacent to coastal parishes whose distance to coastal parishes is less than 20 miles, the frequency for the first category (10-19 miles) is zero for coastal parishes.

We expect, given the very definition of "commuting," that short-distance commuting dominates a majority of all commuting takes place within 30 miles. Table 8 indicates that during the period 1960-90, about 60-70 percent of all commuters traveled from residences that were less than 30 miles away from their place of work.

In 1960 and 1970, the coastal parishes attracted a slightly larger percentage of commuting workers from parishes within 30 miles compared with non-coastal areas, but in 1980 and 1990, they attracted fewer workers from nearby parishes than did non-coastal areas. This pattern becomes even more pronounced when longer commuting distances are considered (see Table 8). In 1960, slightly more workers in non-coastal areas than coastal areas were commuting from 60 miles and beyond (4.0 percent vs. 3.8 percent). Since 1970, however, this pattern has reversed: the percentage of commuting beyond this range in coastal areas compared with non-coastal areas

6

is 6.2 percent versus 3.5 percent (1970), 12.4 percent versus 10.1 percent (1980) and 10.0 percent versus 6.9 percent (1990). Thus, while long-distance commuting has gained more popularity in general in both areas, the coastal areas since 1970 have always topped the non-coastal areas in terms of proportion of workers travelling long-distance. This difference in commuting distance accounts for the greater increase in average commuting distance in coastal areas shown previously in Table 7.

Finally, Tables 9a-9d indicate the parishes (or counties) of origin in terms of source states present for all 11 coastal parishes. As expected from the above analysis, most commuting takes place within Louisiana. Exceptions include Cameron parish bordering Texas and St. Tammany and Orleans which are close to Mississippi.

4.2. Commuting from Adjacent Parishes

While commuting distance expressed in terms of the average straight distance provides an insight into the extent of commuting networks, it might be misleading since a straight distance is often shorter than the actual travel distance measured along the highways. Since a majority of moves take place between parishes located nearby, Table 10 describes the characteristics of commuting in terms of the proportion of commuters in coastal areas from adjacent and nonadjacent parishes.

In general, the proportion of commuters from non-adjacent parishes increased during the period 1960-90, from 17.3 percent in 1960 to 35 percent in 1990. This finding is consistent with the previously shown results showing that commuting distance has increased in general during this period. Most of the shift from adjacent to nonadjacent parishes (or counties) took place during the period 1960-80, for the proportions of commuting from adjacent and nonadjacent parishes remained almost unchanged during the 1980s.

Among coastal parishes, some parishes received far more commuters than others, and proportion of commuting in each coastal parish also changed substantially over time. St. Bernard and St. Mary parishes, in particular, have consistently attracted many more commuters from distant parishes than other coastal parishes during the past 30 years: Seventy-two percent in St. Mary's and 52 percent in St. Bernard's workers in 1990 are commuters from non-adjacent parishes. Cameron and St. Tammany parishes are two other parishes that attracted a large number of commuters from non-adjacent parishes, although the reliance on commuters in Cameron increased after 1970 and that in St. Tammany fluctuated between 1970 and 1990. These four parishes were selected to demonstrate the variation in the source counties of commuters to coastal-area parishes. Some coastal parishes draw commuters mostly from adjacent parishes, whereas other coastal parishes attract commuters from much farther away.

It is not be surprising to find that Cameron and St. Mary attract so many commuters, since major drilling sites are off their coast. St. Bernard, on the other hand, is not a major site, although it does contribute a non-negligible amount of severance tax to the state. Since St. Bernard is developing as part of the New Orleans Metropolitan Area, non-mining related employment opportunities probably induced a significant amount of long-distance commuting.

7

The distinction of source areas in terms of adjacency provides only a crude measure of the geographic spread of commuting networks. The analysis based on total commuting flows may be different from the commuting flow brought about by the mining industry. Thus, we will explore how differences in industrial structure account for differences in commuting patterns between coastal and non-coastal areas for the period 1980-90 for which data on commuting by industry categories are available.

4.3.   Commuting Distance by Industry

The findings presented above suggest that coastal parishes receive commuters from more distant counties than do non-coastal parishes. Since coastal areas are characterized by mining-related activities, at least part of long-distance commuting can be ascribed to the mining industry. Table 11 shows average distance in commuting by industry for coastal and non-coastal areas. The industry "mining" in this table includes, as before, agricultural services, forestry, fisheries and mining. The data in Table 11 show that between 1980 and 1990, the average commuting distance slightly shortened, although the difference between coastal and non-coastal areas in commuting distance increased.

The differentiation of commuting by industry shows that in both 1980 and 1990, mining attracted the longest-distance commuters, and mining workers to coastal parishes traveled much longer distances than those to non-coastal areas. For example, mining workers, regardless of destination, commuted an average of 64.2 miles in 1980 and 59.1 miles in 1990, which is over 20 miles more than traveled by construction workers who also tend to be longer-distance commuters. Furthermore, the comparison of coastal and non-coastal areas reveals that while mining workers commuted the longest distance in both types of areas, their commute to coastal parishes was even longer than to non-coastal parishes.

Tables 12-14 show the distribution of commuters in terms of a 10-mile radius by industry and by coastal and non-coastal area destinations. Table 12 presents the data in terms of mining and non-mining industry for coastal and non-coastal areas for 1980 and 1990. Tables 13 and 14 disaggregate the non-mining industry into more detailed industrial classification. These tables together explain why mining workers to coastal areas, on average, travel a much longer distance than do workers to non-coastal areas.

Table 12 shows that a greater proportion of mining workers than non-mining workers in 1980 and 1990, and in both coastal and non-coastal areas, come from areas located beyond 90 miles (see also Figures 14-15 that graph the data presented in Table 12). In addition, the comparison of coastal and non-coastal parishes indicates that in coastal areas, 27.8 percent of mining workers in 1980 and 25.8 percent in 1990 originate in this farthest location. Less than three percent of coastal-area commuters in all other industries combined came from residences that far away. A differentiation by industry (Tables 13 and 14) shows that the extreme commuting distance is specific to the mining industry in coastal parishes, for no other industry received more than 8 percent of commuters from areas beyond 90 miles away.

Thus, all data presented in the preceding tables clearly indicate that commuting patterns in general, and long-distance commuting in particular, are affected strongly by the combination of two factors: (1) the industry effect, whereby the mining industry attracts relatively more commuters than does any other industry, and (2) location effect, whereby coastal parishes attract relatively more commuters than do non-coastal parishes. Coastal parishes with a heavy dependence on mining, as a result, attract many more long-distance commuters than does mining in non-coastal areas, or than other industries in either type of area.

Finally, Table 15 presents the proportion of mining-related commuters to the 11 coastal parishes from adjoining and nonadjoining parishes. As was shown in Table 10 (for all industries combined), certain parishes within the coastal area attract more commuters than others; these include especially St. Mary, St. Bernard, Cameron, and St. Tammany. The data in Table 15, with the focus on mining employment, clearly show that many more workers are commuting into these parishes from distant locations. On average, more than half of mining-related employment is commuters from non-adjoining parishes, which is very different from the pattern contained in Table 10. Out of 11 coastal parishes, three parishes (St. Bernard, Lafourche, and St. Mary) recruited more than 70 percent of their mining workers from non-adjoining areas, and this proportion is more than 60 percent in Jefferson and Plaquemines. Three parishes, however, received less than 30 percent of their mining workers from non-adjoining places (Iberia, Vermilion and St. Tammany), although this could be a function of the relatively small sample size.

5.   Migration

Migration, just like commuting, can be viewed as an individual response to changing social and economic conditions in the place of origin and destination. Past research has shown that the demographic characteristic of a potential migrant (as well as those of the household in which s/he resides) are likely to be associated with the propensity to migrate. When making the decision to migrate, however, s/he also takes into account the social and economic opportunities available in the area of destination relative to the place of origin. Furthermore, the distance between two places also affects the propensity to migrate.

The opportunity structure that comprises the environment for potential movers varies from area to area, and it could change over time. The discussion above related to commuting patterns suggests that (1) location factor and (2) economic characteristics have independent effects that act simultaneously. It was found that coastal-area location attracts more commuters in general, and more commuters from distant areas in particular. It was also found that, independent of geographic location, an employment structure that relies heavily on mining industry is conducive to a greater number of commuting workers. These findings comprise the theoretical and empirical frame of reference below in which migration patterns are analyzed.

The analysis of migration patterns, however, is more limited in scope due to a lack of several key pieces of information that were available for commuters, such as (1) the occupation of migrants in the place of destination, and (2) migration flow data at county level prior to 1980. Consequently, the analysis of migration patterns prior to 1980, in particular, will be based on net-migration data alone. Migration throughout this report refers to the movement of persons 5 years and older across county lines.

5.1. Migration Patterns 1960-90

Migration generally connects much more distant places than commuting does. This is not surprising, for migration is a (more or less) permanent move of residence, in contrast to daily, weekly, or monthly commuting. Partly because accurate information about distant places is harder to obtain, migration is expected to be less sensitive to a change in social and economic conditions in the sending and receiving areas. Consequently, migration between the areas i and j, once established, is expected to be more stable than that of commuting.

Table 16 indicates that the percentage of migrants in Louisiana has fluctuated within a rather narrow range. The total number of migrants increased from the period 1955-60 to 1975-80 and declined during the period 1985-90. The patterns in coastal and non-coastal areas are similar, although the proportion of migrants in the coastal areas peaked during the period 1965-70, whereas the peak for the non-coastal areas occurred during the period 1975-80. The difference between the two areas in terms of their rates of migration, however, is rather small. The migration rates in the two types of area never differ by more than 2 percent, which is much smaller than the difference observed for commuting (see Table 16).

Migration, compared with commuting, involves a greater number of people from other states. Table 17 disaggregates the migration flow data presented in Table 16 in terms of proximity to the current place of residence. Since detailed migration flow data showing the exact county of origin are not available prior to 1980, the distance is shown only in terms of migration originating in the same state and in other states.

The percent of migration from the same state and other states are fairly evenly divided during the period 1960-1980; in 1990 migration from other states fell to the lowest level in the past 30 years. A similar pattern in trend and level of migration is observed for both the coastal and non-coastal areas which, again, differs from the case of commuting that showed substantial differences between the two types of areas. The overall similarity between coastal and non-coastal areas, however, does not suggest that all parishes in Louisiana experience the same levels of migration; just like commuting, some parishes attract more migration than do others.

5.2. Migration Patterns in Coastal Parishes

Table 18 shows the proportion of out-of-state migrants in the eleven coastal parishes. Four parishes (Jefferson, Orleans, Plaquemines and St. Tammany) attract much more inter-state migrants than do other coastal parishes. While these four parishes are part of the coastal areas that rely so much on oil-related activities, migrants are also likely to be attracted to social and economic opportunities available in metropolitan areas. Jefferson, Orleans and St. Tammany belong to the New Orleans Metropolitan Statistical Area (MSA). Part of the out-of-state migrants to Plaquemines, which borders Orleans, should be also ascribed to the "pull" of the larger metropolitan environment.

Table 19 classifies the place of origin of migrants during the period 1985-90 in terms of adjacency to the current parish of residence. The tabulation in terms of adjacency is only possible for this one period because it requires information on the previous county of residence that is not available for the earlier periods.

Generally, the proportion of migrants from distant counties (non-adjacent areas) is much higher than that of commuters in general (see Table 10). This is an expected result, although the difference becomes much smaller and reversed in some parishes when compared with mining-related commuters (see Table 15).

Five parishes (Orleans, Plaquemines, St. Mary, St. Tammany and Terrebonne) receive migrants from rather distant counties (i.e., non-adjacent counties). Part of the reasons for their reliance on migration is explained by the fact that they either border or are located close to Mississippi. The high proportion of migrants in St.Tammany, in particular, is clearly a function of its closeness to Mississippi. However, as Cameron parish (which borders Texas) shows, closeness to other states alone does not explain why migrants are attracted more to these five parishes, for Cameron parish has a lower than average proportion of migrants. We already noted that of the five parishes with above-average proportions of migration from nonadjacent parishes (or counties), Orleans and St. Tammany belong to the New Orleans MSA, and Plaquemines is located just south of Orleans. Terrebonne belongs to the Houma-Thibodaux MSA, which is a small MSA with a population of less than 200,000. Only St. Mary does not belong to any MSA.

In summary, compared with commuting, coastal and non-coastal areas do not differ much in terms of magnitude of migration and the distance to origin areas. Within the coastal areas, the proportion of long-distance migration appears to be associated with general social and economic opportunities resulting from the proximity to metropolitan areas.

6. Predicting Commuting and Migration

The descriptive analyses presented above clearly indicated that while commuting is closely linked to locational and industrial characteristics, migration is more strongly affected by general economic conditions that are present in the sending and receiving areas. The objective in this section is to quantify the importance of factors considered in the previous sections in a multivariate framework while controlling for the effects of other potentially important factors that may simultaneously affect the pattern of commuting and migration. We will first discuss commuting and migration models, followed by a discussion of the independent variables. The results of the estimates and further discussion will conclude this section.

6.1. Migration and Commuting Models: Three Approaches

Commuting and migration both represent a movement of a person from area i, the place of origin, to j, the destination. However, commuting and migration differ in terms of travel distance and permanency of the movement. Commuting refers to the travel between a person's place of residence and his or her place of work, whereas migration refers to a change in place of residence across county boundaries. The motivation behind the decision for commuting over

11

migration may be quite different, however. While commuting, by definition, is a job-related movement, migration, unless specified as labor migration, may include movements for many non-economic purposes, such as educational and familial movements. Yet commuting and migration are affected by many similar factors (although not to the same extent), and we therefore will discuss both commuting and migration at the same time. We would like to caution, however, that in reality, the decision-making process for commuting may be taking place in a different social and economic context than that of migration.

There are many reviews of migration theories and models, including Greenwood (1975, 1985), Clark (1986), and Cadwallader (1992). However, to our knowledge, few explicit attempts exist for theorizing commuting patterns, even though the impact of commuting on the demographic composition of sending and receiving areas may be as strong as that of migration.

Partly because migration is a subject of concern in many disciplines, various approaches have been put forward in the past several decades regarding the specification of the model and the factors included in the model. In general, past research can be summarized in terms of three general models reflecting different disciplinary concerns: *geographic* models, *economic* models, and *sociological* models. The geographic models emphasize the importance of distance in affecting the volume of migration; economic models emphasize the wage equalizing function of migration between regions as a reflection of an individual's rational behavior to maximize utility; and sociological models emphasize the importance of social networks and social institutional settings that help or hinder movements. These different concerns lead to an emphasis of different factors to be included in the models, and they also resulted in different specifications of the models.

The preoccupation by geographers with spatial effects has led to the adoption of a gravity model which posits that the magnitude of migration is proportional to the product of population in the origin and destination areas and inversely proportional to the distance between them. This type of model is generally specified as:

$$M_{ij} = a \frac{P^{b1}_i P^{b2}_j}{D^{b3}_{ij}} \tag{1}$$

where M_{ij} is the amount of migration between area i and j, P_i and P_j are the populations of area i and j, D_{ij} is the distance between i and j, and a, b_1, and b_2 are parameters to be estimated.

The equation is often linearized by taking the natural logarithm on both sides of equation, and it is estimated using OLS:

$$LogM_{ij} = \log a + b_1 \log P_i + b_2 \log P_j - b_3 \log D_{ij}$$

Past research utilizing this model has consistently found strong evidence supporting the theoretical argument of the gravity model (Cadwallader 1992; Greenwood 1975, 1985; Massey 1989). While the statistical impact of each factor in the gravity model is consistent with its expectations, the interpretation of the results is not clear cut. What do distance and population in

12

origin and destination really mean for an individual decision-maker? And what are the underlying processes that make the product of population in sending and receiving areas have a positive effect on the volume of migration between the two areas?

Distance might represent both economic and psychic costs; it might also lessen the information available to potential migrations about the area of destination and, thereby, reduce the likelihood of migration. Similarly, population may, in fact, reflect social, cultural and economic attraction in the origin and destination. These variables, therefore, are considered to be crude proxies for underlying factors that affect the individual decision-making process. For these reasons, attempts have been made by both economists and geographers to extend the gravity model. That extension generally took the form of explicitly adding economic variables that reflect the economic advantages and disadvantages associated with the areas of origin and destination. The most famous of these extended models, the Lowry model, substituted population with factors related to economic conditions in the place of origin (Lowry 1966). Many other versions of his model have appeared since then. To incorporate the hypothesis that potential migrants compare the characteristics of origin and destination, variables are often expressed either as a ratio or a difference of the value of the variable in the areas of origin and destination. The model is usually expressed as a multiplicative function of origin, destination and distance variables:

$$M_{ij} = a\, D^{b3}_{ij}\, \frac{P_i^{b1}}{P_j^{b2}} \bullet \frac{Y_i^{b3}}{Y_j^{b4}} \tag{2}$$

where M_{ij}, P_i, P_j and D_{ij} are the same as in equation (1), and Y_i and Y_j are the economic variables for sending (i) and receiving (j) areas, such as unemployment rates, percent of workers employed in manufacturing, etc. When linearized, it becomes:

$$\text{Log}M_{ij} = \log a + b_1 \log P_i - b_2 \log P_j + b_3 \log Y_i - b_4 \log Y_j - b_5 \log D_{ij}$$

Instead of using a multiplicative model, a linear-additive model is used occasionally where the model is simply specified as:

$$Mij = a + b_1 Pi + b2 Pj + b3 Yi + b4 Yj + b5\ Dij.$$

It is found, however, that a multiplicative model generally performs better than the linear-additive model.

Finally, sociological models recognize that migration is affected not only by economic factors but also by social conditions such as the presence of family members, relatives and friends in the place of origin and destination which help potential migrants. They create a network of information and social support that tends to positively affect the likelihood that an individual decides to migrate.

$$M_{ij} = a\, D^{b3}_{ij}\, \frac{P_i^{b1}}{P_j^{b2}} \bullet \frac{Y_i^{b3}}{Y_j^{b4}} \bullet \frac{S_i^{b5}}{S_j^{b6}} \tag{3}$$

where M_{ij}, P_i, P_j, D_{ij}, Y_i and Y_j are the same as above and S_i and S_j are the social variables for sending (i) and receiving (j) areas. When linearized, it becomes:

$$LogM_{ij} = \log a + b1 \log P_i - b_2 \log P_j + b_3 \log Y_i - b_4 \log Y_j - b_5 \log S_i - b_6 \log S_j + b_7 \log D_{ij}$$

The existence of such social networks often make it easier for migrants to find a job and a place to live, because these networks often provide information related to jobs, housing and other aspects of the social environment. The assistance may be direct or indirect: direct when the networks share part of the expenses such as providing relocation costs or allowing migrants to stay at their home for free while searching for jobs and housing. The assistance might be indirect if the networks merely provide information regarding jobs and housing. In addition, the presence of such social networks significantly reduces the psychic costs for migrants, i.e. the psychological anxiety when leaving a place in which they are surrounded by familiar faces for a location where they are unknown.

The above description is a rather stylized summary of the migration models and their disciplinary association. Recent models often include all three elements. What they point out is that spatial, social and economic elements are all needed to fully explain the process of migration decision-making if individual-level data are available, and to explain the volume of migration if only aggregate data are available.

6.2   Specification of the Model

While more sophisticated models are available, unavailability of more detailed data restricts our analysis of migration/commuting carried out below to the most enduring, single-equation model.

The past research reviewed above indicates that our model of migration and commuting should include the following variables: distance and factors related to the probability of employment, wage rates, and social networks. The descriptive analyses in earlier sections have also indicated that volume of commuting in the Gulf of Mexico region is affected by proximity to the coastal area. It was further suggested that the fluctuation in oil industry caused by a change in oil prices affected the employment structure after 1974.

In other words, to fully account for the variation in migration and commuting, we should consider spatial and period effects, in addition to three factors above. In the analyses below, we will include factors related to these five aspects as much as possible, although the migration models are much simpler than the commuting models because of a difference between migration and commuting in the availability of detailed data. All models are specified as a multiplicative model as shown in equation (3), and they are estimated using OLS after linearizing the equation.

14

7.   Estimation of the Volume of Commuting and Migration

7.1.   Commuting Model: 1960-1990

Dependent variable:

The dependent variable is the number of persons commuting from area i to j between 1969-70, 1979-80 and 1989-90 regardless of the types of work they are engaged in in the place of work. This type of variable has been normalized in several ways in past migration research (cf. Greenwood and Sweetland 1972). For example, some researchers have normalized it as M_{ij}/P_j, M_{ij}/P_i, or M_{ij}/P_iP_j. These methods of normalization implicitly assume that the population parameters are constrained to one. For example, since

$$\ln(M_{ij}/P_j) = \ln M_{ij} - \ln P_j$$

in a logarithmic form, the regression equation that uses $\ln(M_{ij}/P_j)$ as the dependent variable is equivalent of

$$\ln M_{ij} = \ln a + 1.000 \ln P_j + b_1 \ln Y_i$$

Since there is no *a priori* reason to expect population parameters to be one, we will enter them unconstrained on the right-hand side of the equation for our analysis. The dependent variable in our model, therefore, is the number of (gross) commuters in respective census periods.

Independent variable:

The following independent variables will be considered in the estimation. All the variables except the coastal area location and period dummies are expressed in logarithms:

- The straight distance in mileage between the origin (place of residence) and destination county (place of work).

- Location in coastal parishes in Louisiana: 1 if located in coastal parishes, and 0 otherwise.

- The number of civilian labor force in origin and destination in 1970, 1980 and 1990.

- Percentage of workers in mining industry in 1970, 1980 and 1990.

- Ratio of per capita income in the origin and destination in 1970, 1980 and 1990. The ratio variable is used, instead of entering the per capita income in origin and destination separately, to reduce the magnitude of multicollinearity.

- Unemployment rates in the origin and destination in 1970, 1980 and 1990.

- The number of commuters that took place between the origin and destination in the previous period.

- Period dummy variables to capture the effect of being in 1990 and 1980. The 1970 period is the reference period against which the effect of other periods are compared.

Past migration research has noted the danger of simultaneity bias when the end of (migration) period value is used as the value for independent variables (Greenwood and Sweetland 1972; Greenwood 1975). For example, if the 1980 population is used to predict migration that took place between 1975 and 1980, the possibility exists that the 1980 population is the consequence of migration, rather than the cause of migration. In the analysis of commuting, the use of values close to the time of commuting not only poses fewer problems but may even be desirable. The best solution for this task would be the use of simultaneous equation modeling (SEM); however, the data available for estimating commuting are not suitable for the use of SEM methodology. The second best solution to estimate parameters with less bias would be the use of contemporaneous values, such as the 1980 population, to predict the number of commuters in 1980. To the extent that commuting is measured in terms of a short time-span, the end-of-period value should be very close to what commuters have responded to when they made a decision to commute. On the other hand, the further the date at which the independent variables are measured (even if they precede commuting), the less realistic they would reflect the conditions under which commuting took place. Thus, unless specified otherwise, the independent variables below are generally collected from the same census year in which the data on commuting is reported.

Estimation results:

Table 16 shows, as hypothesized in the previous sections, importance of distance, coastal area location and period effects. The distance, as expected from past research, clearly has a negative effect on the number of commuters. For a one percent increase in mileage between the place of residence and place of work, the number of commuters decreases by 1.1 percent. The location in the coastal region is also shown to increase the number of commuters. The periods effect are also significant. The 1980 period in particular and the 1990 period to a lesser degree increase the number of commuters compared with the 1970 period while controlling for the effect of other variables. As pointed out in Section 3.1, it reiterates the importance of considering the unique effect associated with each period.

The potential commuters not only consider the distance and location but, as economic models argue, compare the economic opportunities in the place of residence and work. Four variables, the percentage of mining, the percentage of manufacturing and construction, unemployment rates and the per capita income, intend to capture the effect of such variables. We expected that the percentage of mining would capture the effect of reliance on mining industry, a peculiar industrial structure in Louisiana, while the percentage of manufacturing and construction would reflect how the difference in the level of more general economic development affect the number of commuters. The effects of both variables, however, are not present. The unemployment rates, which represent the condition in the labor market, are more in line with expectation: a higher unemployment rate in the place of residence sends out more commuters (but not statistically

16

significant) and a higher unemployment rate in the place of work attract less commuters (significant). The only economic variable that has a clear impact on the number of commuters is the ratio of per capita income: a higher income level in the place of work (compared with the place of residence) attracts more commuters.

Lastly, as the sociological model predicts, the presence of friends and relatives who have commuted before is expected to affect the decision of potential commuters. The "stock" variable is at best a crude proxy of the function of social networks. We do not know if previous commuters are still engaged in commuting and are helping the current commuters in the place of work, or they are no longer engaged in commuting (or commuting to different places) but have provided information about the place of work to current commuters. Despite this ambiguity in measurement, the volume of commuters in the previous periods exerts a strong influence on the number of commuters in the current period.

The above results generally confirm the expectation developed in previous sections in a multivariate framework where the effect of a variable is obtained while controlling the effect of others.

It appears, however, that the variables depicting the industrial structure is not very effective for predicting the number of commuters *regardless of their work*. In addition, without incorporating the effect of industry in estimation, we cannot conclude whether or not the difference in commuting distance by industry observed in Section 4 is real. We will address these questions below using more detailed data from the 1980 and 1990 Censuses.

7.2.   Commuting Model: 1980-1990

Dependent variable:

The dependent variable is the number of persons commuting from area i to j between 1989-90. The information about the type of industry engaged by commuters is included in this data.

Independent variable:

In addition to the variables included in the previous section, we will include the six industry dummies and the interaction variables of distance and industry dummies. The definition of industry variables are:

*   Agricultural services, forestry, fisheries and mining.

*   Construction and mining.

*   Transportation, communications, and public utilities.

*   Wholesale and retail trade.

*   Finance, insurance, and real estate.

17

- Services.

Since agricultural services, forestry and fisheries are insignificant in Louisiana, the first industry category largely captures the effect of employment in the mining industry. The reference category to these industry dummy variables is federal, state and local government employees. Self-employed persons, farmers, and persons in military services are excluded. Per capita income in the place of work and residence are entered separately in this exercise, rather than as a ratio variable. Finally, since the dependent variable refers to only one period, the period effect is not included.

Estimation results:

Table 17 shows once again the importance of distance and coastal area location. One percent increase in travel distance reduces the number of commuters by 1.6 percent while coastal area location increases the commuters by 0.3 percent. The interaction of distance and industry dummies demonstrates that the effect of distance indeed varies from industry to industry as observed in Section 4. Among six industries, only the mining industry has a positive effect in the interaction with distance (transportation, communication and public utilities also have a positive coefficient but they are insignificant). Consequently, for a one percent increase in commuting distance, the effect of distance for workers in the mining industry is to decrease commuting by only 0.73% (-1.54 + 0.84) while the effect for workers in the construction and manufacturing industry is to decrease commuting by 2% (-1.57 - 0.44).

Among economic variables, the effect of per capita income is clear where higher income levels in the place of work attract more commuters as found in the previous model. The effect of industrial composition (percent worker in mining and construction/mining), with the presence of industry dummies and industry-distance interactions, become more complex. For example, the percentage of mining workers in the place of residence and work are both positive and significant. The positive effect in the destination confirms our hypothesis since we expected that a greater share of mining industry in terms of employment attracts more commuters. However, a positive effect in the place of residence suggests that a greater share in this industry will actually send out more commuters. Similarly, the effect of construction and mining industry is not only opposite in sign but insignificant. The effect of unemployment rates also has a wrong sign.

The estimation based on more detailed data suggests, therefore, that (1) the commuting networks are geographically more spread for mining workers compared with workers in other industries and (2) the location in coastal areas adds to that effect, but (3) the effect of industrial structure is more mixed. Among economic variables, it is primarily the condition in the labor market (unemployment rates) and the difference in the levels of income in the place of residence and work that are important. The effect of social networks remains strong.

7.3. Migration Model: 1960-1990

Dependent variable:

The first model of migration analyzes the pattern of migration during the period 1960-90. Since migration flow data are not available at county level, the dependent variable in this model is the net migration (in-migration minus out-migration) for the period 1965-70, 1975-80 and 1985-90. Migrants are defined as persons aged 5 years and over whose residence 5 years ago is different from the current residence.

Independent variable:

Similar variables as described in commuting models are used below. However, since the analysis does not distinguish the origin and destination of migrants, all the independent variables refer to social and economic conditions at current parish of residence in Louisiana and distance between the origin and destination counties could not be entered.

Estimation results:

Several specifications were tested and Table 18 shows the result from the final model. Due to a high multicollinearity between the migration stock variable and the size of labor force, and per capita income and period dummy variables, the lag and period variables had to be dropped from the final model.

Unlike the results in the commuting models, the location in coastal areas is not associated with a greater number of migrants; it actually decreases the migration by 0.25%, although it is not statistically significant. Among economic variables, only the per capita income follows our expectation where an increase in income by one percent results in an increase in net-migration by 3.2%. The proportion of workers in the mining industry, in the construction and manufacturing industry and unemployment rates are all significant but to the opposite direction; while a greater share in mining, construction and manufacturing *decreases* the net-migration, a higher unemployment rate actually *increases* it.

The discrepancy between the expectations and this result may be ascribed to several factors. First, since this particular migration data include population aged 5 years and over regardless of their work status, the causes of migration due to non-economic reasons (e.g. marriage, education) may not have been captured by included variables. Second, even if migration occurs for economic reasons, the general labor market conditions such as the area unemployment rates and the proportion of workers in mining and construction/manufacturing industry may not have captured the conditions in a particular industry in which job search is conducted. The final model below intends to address some of these questions.

19

7.4. Migration Model: 1980-1990

Dependent variable:

The dependent variable in the last model is taken from the migration flow files between counties for the period 1985-90. Since information about the age of migrants is included, in this analysis, the sample is restricted to persons aged 25 years and over whose residence in 1990 is different from 1985 so that children and migration for educational reasons are, more or less, excluded.

Independent variable:

In this final analysis, a similar set of variables as used for the analysis of commuting between 1960-90 is used. Since the analysis refers to only one period, the period dummy is not used. In addition, since the migration flow data for the previous period (1975-80) are not available, the lag variable used below is the number of net-migrants that were observed between 1975 and 1980 regardless of their origins.

Estimation results:

The results are generally in line with the findings from the commuting models. It is found that distance, as expected, has a clear negative association with the number of migrants while the location in coastal areas increases migration. Among economic variables, per capita income in destination has a positive and stronger effect than it has in origin, suggesting that a better living standard in the destination attracts more migrants. Similarly, a higher unemployment rates in origin send out more migrants while a higher rates in destination results in lesser migration.

The effect of industrial structure on migration is a little more complex to understand since the parameters for origin and destination variables are both negative. The fact that the effect of construction/mining industry in origin is negative and significant while it is not significant in destination suggests that a higher share in these industries works as a deterrent of migration for the sending communities while the "pull" effect from the destination is largely absent. For the mining industry, the negative effect in both origin and destination indicates that a greater share of workers in this industry discourages migration not only out of origin but into destination communities. It appears that a presence of mining (and other primary) industry in the destination *lowers* the attractiveness of the communities.

Finally, the lag variable, although this is a crude proxy of the effect of prior migration, is again found positive and significant.

In general, as found in the commuting models for 1960-90 and 1980-90, the effect of distance, coastal area location and previous migration have all expected results. The effect of level of living as represented by per capita income in particular and area unemployment rates to a lesser degree affect the migration decision in an expected way. However, the effect of industrial structure does not seem to explain the volume of migration very well. The findings with respect to industrial structure in this respect are, at best, mixed ones.

Figures

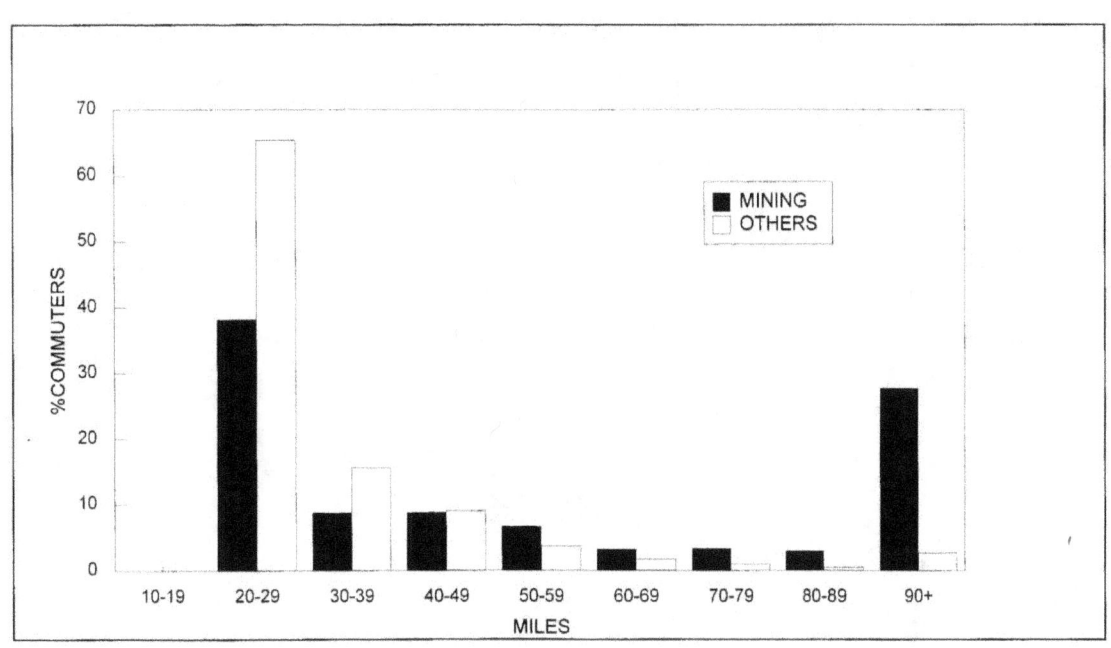

Figure 1. Commuters in Coastal Parishes (%), 1980.

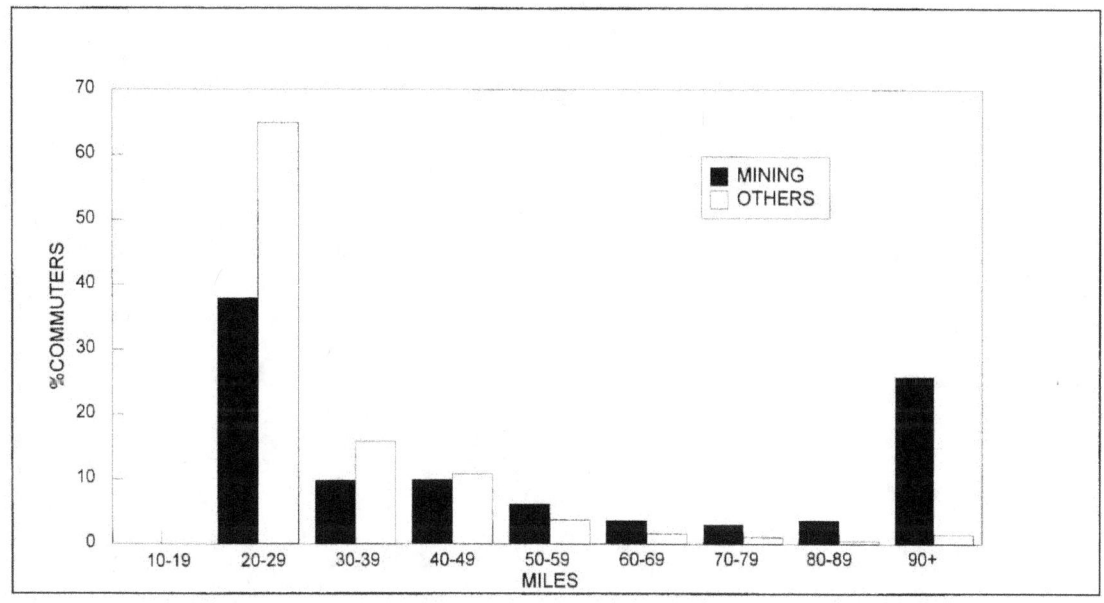

Figure 2. Commuters in Non-Coastal Parishes (%), 1990.

23

Tables

Table 1. Employment in Mining Industry, 1960-90

Employment and Area	Workers 16 yrs+ Mining				Workers Ever Worked Oil/Gas		Workers 16 yrs+ Total				Workers Ever Worked Total	
	1960	1970	1980	1990	1975-80	1985-90	1960	1970	1980	1990	1975-80	1985-90
Number of Workers:												
Total	36,335	46,584	81,327	52,329	89,910	62,457	1,007,812	1,158,245	1,639,394	1,641,614	2,153,907	2,252,845
Non-coastal areas	17,542	22,434	46,167	27,836	52,580	33,874	608,776	686,561	993,006	1,014,405	1,321,862	1,407,219
Coastal areas	18,293	24,150	35,160	24,493	37,330	28,583	399,036	471,684	646,388	627,209	832,045	845,626
% Workers in Mining:												
Total	3.6	4.0	5.0	3.2	4.2	2.8						
Non-coastal areas	2.9	3.3	4.6	2.7	4.0	2.4						
Coastal areas	4.6	5.1	5.4	3.9	4.5	3.4						
%Growth Between Census Periods:												
Total		28.2	74.6	-35.7		-30.5		14.9	41.5	0.1		4.6
Non-coastal areas		25.0	105.8	-39.7		-35.6		12.8	44.6	2.2		6.5
Coastal areas		31.3	45.6	-30.3		-23.4		18.2	37.0	-3.0		1.6
Ratio of Growth Rates of Mining and Total Employment:												
Total		1.9	1.8	-263.3		-6.6						
Non-coastal areas		2.0	2.4	-18.4		-5.5						
Coastal areas		1.7	1.2	10.2		-14.4						

Source: Decennial censuses

27

Table 2. The Number of Parishes by Percentage of
Workers in Mining Industry, 1960-90

Area	%Mining	1960	1970	1980	1990
Non-Coastal Areas	0.0 - 2.5%	29	24	13	29
	2.5 - 5.0%	15	18	24	15
	5.0 -10.0%	7	9	9	7
	10.0%-	2	2	7	2
	Total	53	53	53	53
Coastal Areas	0.0 - 2.5%	3	3	2	3
	2.5 - 5.0%	1	1	2	1
	5.0 -10.0%	1	0	1	3
	10.0%-	6	7	6	4
	Total	11	11	11	11
Total	0.0 - 2.5%	32	27	15	32
	2.5 - 5.0%	16	19	26	16
	5.0 -10.0%	8	9	10	10
	10.0%-	8	9	13	6
	Total	64	64	64	64

Source: Decennial censuses

Table 3. Commuting by Coastal and Non-Coastal Parishes,
1960-90

Employment	Area	1960	1970	1980	1990
Commuters	Coastal	59,709	115,499	196,473	208,513
	Non-coastal	44,776	75,604	183,405	204,092
	Total	104,485	191,103	379,878	412,605
Total Workers	Coastal	370,304	425,670	644,705	642,623
	Non-coastal	572,913	612,732	961,290	987,718
	Total	943,217	1,038,402	1,605,995	1,630,341
%Commuters	Coastal	16	27	30	32
	Non-coastal	7.8	12.3	19.1	20.7
	Total	11.1	18.4	23.7	25.3

Source: Decennial Censuses

Table 4. Growth of Commuting and Percent Commuting by Coastal and
Non-Coastal Parishes, 1960-90

		1960-70	1970-80	1980-90
COMMUTERS	COAST	93.4	70.1	6.1
	NONCOAST	68.8	142.6	11.3
	TOTAL	82.9	98.8	8.6
TOTAL WORKERS	COAST	15.0	51.5	-0.3
	NONCOAST	7.0	56.9	2.7
	TOTAL	10.1	54.7	1.5

Source: Decennial Censuses

Table 5. Commuters and Total Workers by Industry and Coastal/Non-Coastal Parishes, 1980-90

Industry	Total Workers 1980			Total Workers 1990			Commuters 1980			Commuters 1990		
	Total	Coast	Noncoast	Total	Coast	Noncoast	Total	Coast	Noncoast	Total	Coast	Noncoast
Total	1,442,845	591,045	851,800	1,449,889	583,414	866,475	339,641	178,448	161,193	364,650	188,409	176,241
Agri. services, forestry, fisheries, Mining	76,756	39,017	37,739	54,920	30,432	24,488	29,809	18,369	11,440	23,512	15,960	7,552
Construction	119,335	43,529	75,806	81,040	29,305	51,735	45,820	18,721	27,099	31,347	12,515	18,832
Manufacturing	214,691	72,682	142,009	188,300	57,946	130,354	65,533	27,946	37,587	65,241	23,914	41,327
Transp, communication, pub. utils.	106,352	56,053	50,299	94,574	44,014	50,560	33,822	21,128	12,694	32,890	19,064	13,826
Wholesale, retail trade	304,780	129,773	175,007	325,054	136,140	188,914	55,620	31,663	23,957	67,592	36,518	31,074
Finance, Insurance, real estate	72,486	31,673	40,813	80,270	35,421	44,849	14,430	9,746	4,684	18,309	11,975	6,334
Services	255,674	116,078	139,596	342,120	153,115	189,005	45,863	28,366	17,497	73,925	44,821	29,104
Federal government	51,370	23,071	28,299	49,031	21,845	27,186	13,196	8,088	5,108	14,096	8,691	5,405
State, local government	241,401	79,169	162,232	234,580	75,196	159,384	35,548	14,421	21,127	37,738	14,951	22,787

Source: Decennial Censuses

29

Table 6. Percent Commuters by Industry and Coastal/Non-Coastal Parishes, 1980-90

Industry	%Commuters 1980			%Commuters 1990		
	Total	Coast	Non-coast	Total	Coast	Non-coast
Total	23.5	30.2	18.9	25.2	32.3	20.3
Agri. services, forestry, fisheries, Mining	38.8	47.1	30.3	42.8	52.4	30.8
Construction	38.4	43.0	35.7	38.7	42.7	36.4
Manufacturing	30.5	38.4	26.5	34.6	41.3	31.7
Transp, communication, pub. utils.	31.8	37.7	25.2	34.8	43.3	27.3
Wholesale, retail trade	18.2	24.4	13.7	20.8	26.8	16.4
Finance, Insurance, real estate	19.9	30.8	11.5	22.8	33.8	14.1
Services	17.9	24.4	12.5	21.6	29.3	15.4
Federal government	25.7	35.1	18.1	28.7	39.8	19.9
State, local government	14.7	18.2	13.0	16.1	19.9	14.3

Source: Decennial Censuses

Table 7. Average Commuting Distance: Coastal and Non-Coastal Parishes, 1960-90

(Mile)

Area	1960	1970	1980	1990
Total	32.3	32.1	42.3	38.6
Non-coastal area	30.1	28.5	36.9	32.5
Coastal area	34.0	34.5	47.4	44.5

%Growth in Commuting Distance			
	1960-70	1970-80	1980-90
Total	-0.6	31.8	-9.0
Non-coastal area	-5.2	29.4	-12.0
Coastal area	1.5	37.6	-6.2

Source: Decennial Censuses

Table 8. Commuting in Coastal and Non-Coastal Areas, 1960-90

1960

Area		10-19	20-29	30-39	40-49	50-59	60-69	70-79	80-89	90+	Other	Total
						Miles						
Non-coastal	N	10,853	17,967	9,646	3,406	1,123	470	473	170	668	0	44,776
	%	24.2	40.1	21.5	7.6	2.5	1.1	1.1	0.4	1.5	0.0	100.0
Coastal	N	0	41,200	9,886	3,201	3,170	865	358	234	699	96	59,709
	%	0.0	69.0	16.6	5.4	5.3	1.5	0.6	0.4	1.2	0.2	100.0

1970

Area		10-19	20-29	30-39	40-49	50-59	60-69	70-79	80-89	90+	Other	Total
						Miles						
Non-coastal	N	18,760	31,194	16,514	4,329	2,151	1,173	830	525	128	0	75,604
	%	24.8	41.3	21.8	5.7	2.9	1.6	1.1	0.7	0.2	0.0	100.0
Coastal	N	0	78,626	16,230	8,866	4,666	1,177	1,123	3,177	1,634	0	115,499
	%	0.0	68.1	14.1	7.7	4.0	1.0	1.0	2.8	1.4	0.0	100.0

1980

Area		10-19	20-29	30-39	40-49	50-59	60-69	70-79	80-89	90+	Other	Total
						Miles						
Non-coastal	N	38,519	75,018	36,937	9,458	4,871	3,294	2,649	3,096	9,563	0	183,405
	%	21.0	40.9	20.1	5.2	2.7	1.8	1.4	1.7	5.2	0.0	100.0
Coastal	N	0	118,054	28,409	17,468	8,199	4,088	2,824	1,803	15,604	24	196,473
	%	0.0	60.1	14.5	8.9	4.2	2.1	1.4	0.9	7.9	0.0	100.0

1990

Area		10-19	20-29	30-39	40-49	50-59	60-69	70-79	80-89	90+	Other	Total
						Miles						
Non-coastal	N	43,510	87,850	42,006	11,812	4,809	3,460	2,679	2,199	5,767	0	204,092
	%	21.3	43.0	20.6	5.8	2.4	1.7	1.3	1.1	2.8	0.0	100.0
Coastal	N	0	124,914	30,865	21,955	8,846	4,056	2,944	2,087	12,833	13	208,513
	%	0.0	59.9	14.8	10.5	4.2	2.0	1.4	1.0	6.2	0.0	100.0

Source: Decennial Censuses

31

Table 9a. Commuting Patterns by Sending States, 1960

Receiving Parishes	Sending States												
	Louisiana		Alabama		Florida		Mississippi		Texas		Other states		Total	
	N	%	N	%	N	%	N	%	N	%	N	%	N	%
Total	57,949	97.1	95	0.2	0	0.0	1,141	1.9	346	0.6	178	0.3	59,709	100.0
Cameron	654	91.0	0	0.0	0	0.0	0	0.0	65	9.0	0	0.0	719	100.0
Iberia	937	100.0	0	0.0	0	0.0	0	0.0	0	0.0	0	0.0	937	100.0
Jefferson	9,912	98.0	0	0.0	0	0.0	163	2.0	0	0.0	0	0.0	10,075	100.0
Lafourche	1,215	100.0	0	0.0	0	0.0	0	0.0	0	0.0	0	0.0	1,215	100.0
Orleans	35,710	96.3	95	0.3	0	0.0	811	2.2	281	0.8	178	0.5	37,075	100.0
Plaquemines	2,247	100.0	0	0.0	0	0.0	0	0.0	0	0.0	0	0.0	2,247	100.0
St. Bernard	2,620	99.0	0	0.0	0	0.0	32	1.0	0	0.0	0	0.0	2,652	100.0
St. Mary	2,240	100.0	0	0.0	0	0.0	0	0.0	0	0.0	0	0.0	2,240	100.0
St. Tammany	524	80.0	0	0.0	0	0.0	135	20.0	0	0.0	0	0.0	659	100.0
Terrebonne	1,210	100.0	0	0.0	0	0.0	0	0.0	0	0.0	0	0.0	1,210	100.0
Vermilion	680	100.0	0	0.0	0	0.0	0	0.0	0	0.0	0	0.0	680	100.0

Source: Decennial Censuses

Table 9b. Commuting Patterns by Sending States, 1970

Receiving Parishes	Sending States												
	Louisiana		Alabama		Florida		Mississippi		Texas		Other states		Total	
	N	%	N	%	N	%	N	%	N	%	N	%	N	%
Total	113,045	97.9	417	0.4	0	0.0	1,668	1.4	369	0.3	0	0.0	115,499	100.0
Cameron	419	87.0	0	0.0	0	0.0	0	0.0	65	13.0	0	0.0	484	100.0
Iberia	1,899	100.0	0	0.0	0	0.0	0	0.0	0	0.0	0	0.0	1,899	100.0
Jefferson	30,546	99.0	0	0.0	0	0.0	241	1.0	0	0.0	0	0.0	30,787	100.0
Lafourche	1,418	100.0	0	0.0	0	0.0	0	0.0	0	0.0	0	0.0	1,418	100.0
Orleans	63,714	97.0	417	1.0	0	0.0	1,105	2.0	304	0.0	0	0.0	65,540	100.0
Plaquemines	3,657	100.0	0	0.0	0	0.0	0	0.0	0	0.0	0	0.0	3,657	100.0
St. Bernard	3,330	99.0	0	0.0	0	0.0	31	1.0	0	0.0	0	0.0	3,361	100.0
St. Mary	3,411	100.0	0	0.0	0	0.0	0	0.0	0	0.0	0	0.0	3,411	100.0
St. Tammany	2,081	88.0	0	0.0	0	0.0	291	12.0	0	0.0	0	0.0	2,372	100.0
Terrebonne	1,910	100.0	0	0.0	0	0.0	0	0.0	0	0.0	0	0.0	1,910	100.0
Vermilion	660	100.0	0	0.0	0	0.0	0	0.0	0	0.0	0	0.0	660	100.0

Source: Decennial Censuses

Table 9c. Commuting Patterns by Sending States, 1980

Receiving Parishes	Sending states													
	Louisiana		Alabama		Florida		Mississippi		Texas		Other states		Total	
	N	%	N	%	N	%	N	%	N	%	N	%	N	%
Total	183,330	93.3	1,284	0.7	1,266	0.6	8,074	4.1	1,437	0.7	1,082	0.6	196,473	100.0
Cameron	2,168	82.0	54	2.0	0	0.0	97	4.0	268	10.0	48	1.8	2,635	100.0
Iberia	5,417	100.0	0	0.0	21	0.0	0	0.0	0	0.0	0	0.0	5,438	100.0
Jefferson	41,131	95.0	260	1.0	330	1.0	1,428	3.0	140	0.0	133	0.3	43,422	100.0
Lafourche	3,133	95.0	35	1.0	13	0.0	15	0.5	47	2.0	40	1.2	3,283	100.0
Orleans	93,716	94.0	462	0.5	363	0.0	3,283	3.0	839	0.8	861	0.9	99,524	100.0
Plaquemines	9,294	90.0	190	2.0	56	1.0	738	7.0	0	0.0	0	0.0	10,278	100.0
St. Bernard	5,119	95.0	0	0.0	0	0.0	250	5.0	0	0.0	0	0.0	5,369	100.0
St. Mary	10,419	89.0	196	2.0	317	3.0	712	6.0	122	1.0	0	0.0	11,766	100.0
St. Tammany	2,736	70.0	16	0.0	45	1.0	1,134	29.0	0	0.0	0	0.0	3,931	100.0
Terrebonne	7,537	92.0	71	1.0	121	1.0	413	5.0	21	0.0	0	0.0	8,163	100.0
Vermilion	2,660	100.0	0	0.0	0	0.0	4	0.0	0	0.0	0	0.0	2,664	100.0

Source: Decennial Censuses

Table 9d. Commuting Patterns by Sending States, 1990

Receiving Parishes	Sending states													
	Louisiana		Alabama		Florida		Mississippi		Texas		Other states		Total	
	N	%	N	%	N	%	N	%	N	%	N	%	N	%
Total	195,544	93.8	968	0.5	937	0.4	9,037	4.3	1,338	0.6	689	0.3	208,513	100.0
Cameron	1,988	82.0	16	1.0	61	2.0	75	3.0	278	12.0	0	0.0	2,418	100.0
Iberia	4,774	99.0	20	0.0	25	1.0	0	0.0	0	0.0	0	0.0	4,819	100.0
Jefferson	52,387	96.0	193	0.0	130	0.0	1,594	3.0	314	1.0	15	0.0	54,633	100.0
Lafourche	3,840	95.0	17	0.0	56	1.0	126	3.0	0	0.0	0	0.0	4,039	100.0
Orleans	97,353	94.0	395	0.0	385	0.0	3,623	4.0	639	1.0	674	0.7	103,069	100.0
Plaquemines	9,631	90.0	141	1.0	67	1.0	751	7.0	61	1.0	0	0.0	10,651	100.0
St. Bernard	3,616	92.0	0	0.0	0	0.0	299	8.0	0	0.0	0	0.0	3,915	100.0
St. Mary	8,452	92.0	117	1.0	123	1.0	474	5.0	26	0.0	0	0.0	9,192	100.0
St. Tammany	4,143	70.0	27	0.0	0	0.0	1,734	29.0	0	0.0	0	0.0	5,904	100.0
Terrebonne	6,941	94.0	42	1.0	90	1.0	310	4.0	20	0.0	0	0.0	7,403	100.0
Vermilion	2,419	98.0	0	0.0	0	0.0	51	2.0	0	0.0	0	0.0	2,470	100.0

Source: Decennial Censuses

33

Table 10. Commuting Patterns to Coastal Parishes, 1960-90

	Commuters							
Area	1960		1970		1980		1990	
	N	%	N	%	N	%	N	%
All Parishes								
Total	59,709	100.0	115,499	100.0	196,473	100.0	208,513	100.0
Adj. Parishes	50,637	82.8	93,290	76.1	141,618	65.8	142,106	65.0
Non-Adj. Parishes	9,072	17.3	22,209	23.9	54,855	34.3	66,407	35.0
Cameron								
Total	719	100.0	484	100.0	2,635	100.0	2,418	100.0
Adj. Parishes	659	91.7	388	80.2	1,249	47.4	1,315	54.4
Non-Adj. Parishes	60	8.3	96	19.8	1,386	52.6	1,103	45.6
Iberia								
Total	937	100.0	1,899	100.0	5,438	100.0	4,819	100.0
Adj. Parishes	926	98.8	1,780	93.7	4,692	86.3	4,364	90.6
Non-Adj. Parishes	11	1.2	119	6.3	746	13.7	455	9.4
Jefferson								
Total	10,075	100.0	30,787	100.0	43,422	100.0	54,633	100.0
Adj. Parishes	8,562	85.0	23,206	75.4	31,607	72.8	35,356	64.7
Non-Adj. Parishes	1,513	15.0	7,581	24.6	11,815	27.2	19,277	35.3
La Fourche								
Total	1,215	100.0	1,418	100.0	3,283	100.0	4,039	100.0
Adj. Parishes	1,083	89.1	1,237	87.2	2,434	74.1	3,067	75.9
Non-Adj. Parishes	132	11.0	181	13.0	849	26.0	972	24.0
Orleans								
Total	37,075	100.0	65,540	100.0	99,524	100.0	103,069	100.0
Adj. Parishes	32,422	87.4	56,348	86.0	78,065	78.4	75,184	72.9
Non-Adj. Parishes	4,653	12.5	9,192	14.0	21,459	21.6	27,885	27.1
Plaquemines								
Total	2,247	100.0	3,657	100.0	10,278	100.0	10,651	100.0
Adj. Parishes	1,935	86.1	3,149	86.1	7,883	76.7	7,452	70.0
Non-Adj. Parishes	312	13.9	508	13.9	2,395	23.3	3,199	30.0
St. Bernard								
Total	2,652	100.0	3,361	100.0	5,369	100.0	3,915	100.0
Adj. Parishes	1,795	67.7	2,195	65.3	2,818	52.5	1,867	47.7
Non-Adj. Parishes	857	32.3	1,166	34.7	2,551	47.5	2,048	52.3
St. Mary								
Total	2,240	100.0	3,411	100.0	11,766	100.0	9,192	100.0
Adj. Parishes	1,136	50.7	1,783	52.3	2,593	22.0	2,533	27.6
Non-Adj. Parishes	1,104	49.3	1,628	47.7	9,173	78.0	6,659	72.4
St. Tammany								
Total	659	100.0	2,372	100.0	3,931	100.0	5,904	100.0
Adj. Parishes	578	87.7	1,085	45.7	2,648	67.4	3,642	61.7
Non-Adj. Parishes	81	12.3	1,287	54.3	1,283	32.6	2,262	38.3
Terrebonne								
Total	1,210	100.0	1,910	100.0	8,163	100.0	7,403	100.0
Adj. Parishes	940	77.7	1,567	82.0	5,562	68.1	5,435	73.4
Non-Adj. Parishes	270	22.3	343	18.0	2,601	31.9	1,968	26.6
Vermilion								
Total	680	100.0	660	100.0	2,664	100.0	2,470	100.0
Adj. Parishes	601	88.4	552	83.6	2,067	77.6	1,891	76.6
Non-Adj. Parishes	79	11.6	108	16.4	597	22.4	579	23.4

Source: Decennial Censuses

Table 11. Average Commuting Distance by Industry

(MILE)

Industry	1980			1990		
	Total	Coast	Non-coast	Total	Coast	Non-coast
Total	42.3	47.4	36.9	38.6	44.5	32.5
Agri. services, forestry, fisheries, Mining	64.2	70.8	53.5	59.1	68.0	40.3
Construction	41.5	46.7	37.9	38.0	41.8	35.5
Manufacturing	33.8	37.3	31.2	30.7	34.9	28.3
Transp, communication, pub. utils.	37.0	39.6	32.8	34.2	38.4	28.5
Wholesale, retail trade	32.4	34.0	30.3	30.6	33.0	27.8
Finance, Insurance, real estate	29.5	29.4	29.6	28.3	30.3	24.5
Services	32.9	33.3	32.3	30.5	32.4	27.5
Federal government	29.9	29.8	30.1	39.3	47.7	25.8
State, local government	32.0	33.0	31.2	30.4	32.3	29.1

Source: Decennial Censuses

Table 12. Commuters by Travel Distance, 1980 and 1990 (%)

Area	Industry	Miles									Total
		10-19	20-29	30-39	40-49	50-59	60-69	70-79	80-89	90+	
1980											
Non-Coast	Mining	11.9	32.8	19.6	6.8	4.1	2.7	2.8	3.3	15.9	100.0
	Others	23.0	43.3	20.1	4.2	2.0	1.4	1.1	1.5	3.4	100.0
Coast	Mining	0.0	38.3	8.8	8.9	6.7	3.3	3.4	3.0	27.8	100.0
	Others	0.0	65.4	15.7	9.1	3.8	1.8	1.0	0.5	2.7	100.0
1990											
Non-Coast	Mining	10.4	39.8	26.3	5.9	3.3	1.2	2.8	2.0	8.3	100.0
	Others	23.7	45.7	20.5	4.8	1.5	1.2	0.8	0.8	1.0	100.0
Coast	Mining	0.0	37.9	9.8	9.9	6.2	3.6	3.0	3.7	25.8	100.0
	Others	0.0	64.9	15.8	10.9	3.8	1.6	1.1	0.5	1.5	100.0

Source: Decennial Censuses

Table 13. Distribution of Commuters by Travel Distance by Industry in Coastal and Non-Coastal Areas, 1980 (%)

| Non-Coastal Area | Miles | | | | | | | | | |
Industry	10-19	20-29	30-39	40-49	50-59	60-69	70-79	80-89	90+	Total
Total	22.3	42.6	20.1	4.4	2.1	1.4	1.2	1.6	4.3	100.0
Agri. services, forestry, fisheries, Mining	11.9	32.8	19.6	6.8	4.1	2.7	2.8	3.3	15.9	100.0
Construction	13.3	40.5	22.5	7.3	4.5	2.9	1.4	2.8	4.8	100.0
Manufacturing	21.5	48.5	19.1	4.3	1.3	0.8	0.6	1.0	2.9	100.0
Transp, communication, pub. utils.	26.7	38.7	21.2	3.5	2.0	1.1	1.2	1.5	4.2	100.0
Wholesale, retail trade	29.1	41.8	18.3	3.1	1.3	1.1	1.1	1.8	2.6	100.0
Finance, Insurance, real estate	31.9	47.2	13.4	1.8	0.9	0.0	0.0	0.0	4.8	100.0
Services	29.8	41.2	16.7	2.7	1.6	1.2	1.6	1.6	3.7	100.0
Federal government	34.9	27.0	30.2	2.2	1.2	0.0	1.1	0.3	3.2	100.0
State, local government	20.1	48.3	19.2	4.3	2.0	1.3	1.2	1.1	2.5	100.0
Coastal Area										
Total	0.0	62.8	15.0	9.1	4.0	1.9	1.2	0.8	5.1	100.0
Agri. services, forestry, fisheries, Mining	0.0	38.3	8.8	8.9	6.7	3.3	3.4	3.0	27.8	100.0
Construction	0.0	49.2	14.7	16.5	4.4	4.3	2.2	1.5	7.1	100.0
Manufacturing	0.0	52.5	21.6	11.3	6.5	3.2	1.5	1.1	2.3	100.0
Transp, communication, pub. utils.	0.0	61.4	18.1	7.4	4.0	1.8	1.5	0.6	5.3	100.0
Wholesale, retail trade	0.0	71.8	14.0	8.6	2.3	1.1	0.7	0.1	1.4	100.0
Finance, Insurance, real estate	0.0	78.5	15.0	5.3	0.7	0.0	0.1	0.1	0.3	100.0
Services	0.0	75.7	12.6	7.0	2.2	0.7	0.4	0.3	1.1	100.0
Federal government	0.0	74.7	16.4	4.3	3.6	0.1	0.6	0.0	0.2	100.0
State, local government	0.0	70.5	14.4	7.8	3.8	1.2	0.4	0.0	2.0	100.0

Source: 1980 Census

Table 14. Distribution of Commuters by Travel Distance by Industry in Coastal and Non-Coastal Areas, 1990 (%)

Non-Coastal Area	Miles									
Industry	10-19	20-29	30-39	40-49	50-59	60-69	70-79	80-89	90+	Total
Total	23.2	45.4	20.7	4.8	1.6	1.2	0.9	0.9	1.3	100.0
Agri. services, forestry, fisheries, Mining	10.4	39.8	26.3	5.9	3.3	1.2	2.8	2.0	8.3	100.0
Construction	15.1	41.5	19.2	10.6	4.4	2.7	1.6	2.1	2.8	100.0
Manufacturing	21.5	48.8	20.4	5.6	1.4	0.9	0.4	0.4	0.6	100.0
Transp, communication, pub. utils.	24.1	42.8	23.2	4.1	2.0	1.2	1.0	0.4	1.3	100.0
Wholesale, retail trade	27.1	45.8	18.5	3.7	1.1	1.1	0.7	0.9	1.0	100.0
Finance, Insurance, real estate	29.6	49.6	18.4	1.0	0.0	0.8	0.0	0.5	0.0	100.0
Services	25.7	47.0	19.4	3.3	1.2	1.1	1.0	0.9	0.5	100.0
Federal government	40.3	29.2	24.6	3.8	1.1	0.4	0.2	0.4	0.0	100.0
State, local government	18.7	50.5	21.1	4.1	0.7	1.7	1.3	0.9	1.0	100.0
Coastal Area										
Total	0.0	62.7	15.3	10.8	4.0	1.8	1.2	0.8	3.4	100.0
Agri. services, forestry, fisheries, Mining	0.0	37.9	9.8	9.9	6.2	3.6	3.0	3.7	25.8	100.0
Construction	0.0	45.1	17.5	17.6	7.9	4.1	2.1	1.3	4.4	100.0
Manufacturing	0.0	53.5	20.7	13.6	6.2	2.9	1.3	0.6	1.1	100.0
Transp, communication, pub. utils.	0.0	62.1	15.9	9.1	4.0	1.8	2.3	0.3	4.6	100.0
Wholesale, retail trade	0.0	65.4	16.4	11.4	2.6	1.6	0.9	0.5	1.2	100.0
Finance, Insurance, real estate	0.0	73.1	13.3	11.6	1.2	0.3	0.2	0.2	0.0	100.0
Services	0.0	72.0	13.8	9.0	2.5	0.9	0.6	0.5	0.7	100.0
Federal government	0.0	71.8	13.8	8.4	4.1	0.6	0.9	0.0	0.4	100.0
State, local government	0.0	69.5	16.5	7.6	3.1	1.1	1.1	0.4	0.6	100.0

Source: 1990 Census

Table 15.   Commuting Patterns Related to Mining Industries in Coastal Parishes, 1980 and 1990

	1980		1990	
	N	%	N	%
All Parishes				
Total	18,369	100.0	15,960	100.0
Adj. Parishes	8,950	48.7	7,056	44.2
Non-Adj. Parishes	9,419	51.3	8,904	55.8
Cameron				
Total	1,401	100.0	905	100.0
Adj. Parishes	438	31.3	378	41.8
Non-Adj. Parishes	963	68.7	527	58.2
Iberia				
Total	879	100.0	781	100.0
Adj. Parishes	701	79.7	602	77.1
Non-Adj. Parishes	178	20.3	179	22.9
Jefferson				
Total	2,373	100.0	2,029	100.0
Adj. Parishes	917	38.6	654	32.2
Non-Adj. Parishes	1,456	61.4	1,375	67.8
La Fourche				
Total	330	100.0	527	100.0
Adj. Parishes	158	47.9	146	27.7
Non-Adj. Parishes	172	52.1	381	72.3
Orleans				
Total	6,066	100.0	5,476	100.0
Adj. Parishes	3,806	62.7	2,580	47.1
Non-Adj. Parishes	2,260	37.3	2,896	52.9
Plaquemines				
Total	1,886	100.0	1,860	100.0
Adj. Parishes	1,006	53.3	733	39.4
Non-Adj. Parishes	880	46.7	1,127	60.6
St. Bernard				
Total	36	100.0	117	100.0
Adj. Parishes	0	0.0	25	21.4
Non-Adj. Parishes	36	100.0	92	78.6
St. Mary				
Total	2,984	100.0	2,169	100.0
Adj. Parishes	659	22.1	631	29.1
Non-Adj. Parishes	2,325	77.9	1,538	70.9
St. Tammany				
Total	56	100.0	69	100.0
Adj. Parishes	56	100.0	49	71.0
Non-Adj. Parishes	0	0.0	20	29.0
Terrebonne				
Total	1,666	100.0	1,444	100.0
Adj. Parishes	729	43.8	828	57.3
Non-Adj. Parishes	937	56.2	616	42.7
Vermilion				
Total	692	100.0	583	100.0
Adj. Parishes	480	69.4	430	73.8
Non-Adj. Parishes	212	30.6	153	26.2

Source: Decennial Censuses

Table 16.   Migration to Coastal And Non-Coastal Parishes, 1960-90

	Area	1955-60	1965-70	1975-80	1985-90
Migrant	Coast	161,463	219,886	241,363	190,147
	Noncoast	290,247	353,874	435,309	372,554
	Total	451,710	573,760	676,672	562,701
Total	Coast	1,029,490	1,237,070	1,424,033	1,418,101
	Noncoast	1,785,332	2,027,816	2,379,212	2,438,054
	Total	2,814,822	3,264,886	3,803,245	3,856,155
%Migrant	Coast	15.7	17.8	16.9	13.4
	Noncoast	16.3	17.5	18.3	15.3
	Total	16.0	17.6	17.8	14.6

Note: Migrants exclude persons from abroad.
Source: Decennial Censuses

Table 17. Migration to Coastal and Non-Coastal Areas by Origin State, 1960-90

	1960		1970		1980		1990	
	N	%	N	%	N	%	N	%
Non-migrants	2,363,111	84.0	2,691,125	82.4	3,126,573	82.2	3,293,454	85.4
Migrants	451,710	16.0	573,760	17.6	676,672	17.8	562,701	14.6
From the same state	248,763	8.8	269,736	8.3	352,006	9.3	337,349	8.7
From other states	202,947	7.2	304,024	9.3	324,666	8.5	225,352	5.8
Total	2,814,822	100.0	3,264,886	100.0	3,803,245	100.0	3,856,155	100.0
Coastal Area								
Non-migrants	868,027	84.3	1,017,184	82.2	1,182,670	83.1	1,227,954	86.6
Migrants	161,463	15.7	219,886	17.8	241,363	16.9	190,147	13.4
From the same state	90,037	8.7	109,139	8.8	121,468	8.5	114,397	8.1
From other states	71,426	6.9	110,747	9.0	119,895	8.4	75,750	5.3
Total	1,029,490	100.0	1,237,070	100.0	1,424,033	100.0	1,418,101	100.0
Non-Coastal Area								
Non-migrants	1,495,084	83.7	1,673,942	82.5	1,943,903	81.7	2,065,500	84.7
Migrants	290,247	16.3	353,874	17.5	435,309	18.3	372,554	15.3
From the same state	158,726	8.9	160,597	7.9	230,538	9.7	222,952	9.1
From other states	131,521	7.4	193,277	9.5	204,771	8.6	149,602	6.1
Total	1,785,332	173.4	2,027,816	163.9	2,379,212	167.1	2,438,054	171.9

Note: Migration excludes persons from abroad.

Source: Decennial Censuses

40

Table 18. Percent of Population Migrating from Other States
to Coastal Parishes, 1960-90

Area	1960	1970	1980	1990
Cameron	6.3	8.1	8.0	3.6
Iberia	5.7	3.3	4.6	2.4
Jefferson	9.1	9.3	9.8	5.2
Lafourche	3.5	2.9	4.0	2.0
Orleans	6.7	7.4	8.1	6.5
Plaquemines	10.6	8.9	11.3	7.2
St. Bernard	5.0	4.1	2.5	2.1
St. Mary	6.7	6.1	6.8	3.1
St. Tammany	7.0	13.6	15.9	10.1
Terrebonne	6.1	5.0	6.7	2.5
Vermilion	2.7	2.2	2.9	1.9

Source: Decennial Censuses

Table 19. Migration to Coastal Parishes, 1990

Area	Migrants N	%
All Parishes		
Total	190,147	100.0
Adj. Parishes	60,374	39.0
Non-Adj. Parishes	129,773	61.0
Cameron		
Total	1,160	100.0
Adj. Parishes	672	57.9
Non-Adj. Parishes	488	42.1
Iberia		
Total	4,814	100.0
Adj. Parishes	2,184	45.4
Non-Adj. Parishes	2,630	54.6
Jefferson		
Total	62,908	100.0
Adj. Parishes	28,866	45.9
Non-Adj. Parishes	34,042	54.1
Lafourche		
Total	7,884	100.0
Adj. Parishes	4,103	52.0
Non-Adj. Parishes	3,781	48.0
Orleans		
Total	53,587	100.0
Adj. Parishes	11,808	22.0
Non-Adj. Parishes	41,779	78.0
Plaquemines		
Total	4,048	100.0
Adj. Parishes	1,595	39.4
Non-Adj. Parishes	2,453	60.6
St. Bernard		
Total	6,321	100.0
Adj. Parishes	3,243	51.3
Non-Adj. Parishes	3,078	48.7
St. Mary		
Total	4,453	100.0
Adj. Parishes	1,113	25.0
Non-Adj. Parishes	3,340	75.0
St. Tammany		
Total	33,973	100.0
Adj. Parishes	2,415	7.1
Non-Adj. Parishes	31,558	92.9
Terrebonne		
Total	7,431	100.0
Adj. Parishes	2,713	36.5
Non-Adj. Parishes	4,718	63.5
Vermilion		
Total	3,568	100.0
Adj. Parishes	1,662	46.6
Non-Adj. Parishes	1,906	53.4

Note: Excludes persons from abroad.
Source: 1990 Census

Bibliography

Cadwallader, M. 1992. *Migration and Residential Mobility: Macro and Micro Approaches.* Madison: The University of Wisconsin Press

Clark, W. A. V. 1986. *Human Migration.* Beverly Hills: Sage Publications.

Greenwood, M. J. 1975. "Research on Internal Migration in the United States: A Survey." *Journal of Economic Literature* 13: 397-433.

Greenwood, M. J. 1985. "Human Migration: Theory, Models, and Empirical Studies." *Journal of Regional Science* 25: 521-544.

Greenwood, M. J. and D. Sweetland. 1972. "The Determinants of Migration between Standard Metropolitan Statistical Areas." Demography 9(4): 665-681.

Lowry, I. 1966. Migration and Metropolitan Growth: Two Analytical Models. San Francisco: Chandler.

Massey, D. S. 1990. "Social Structure, Household Strategies, and the Cumulative Causation of Migration." *Population Index* 56(1): 3-26.

The Department of the Interior Mission

As the Nation's principal conservation agency, the Department of the Interior has responsibility for most of our nationally owned public lands and natural resources. This includes fostering sound use of our land and water resources; protecting our fish, wildlife, and biological diversity; preserving the environmental and cultural values of our national parks and historical places; and providing for the enjoyment of life through outdoor recreation. The Department assesses our energy and mineral resources and works to ensure that their development is in the best interests of all our people by encouraging stewardship and citizen participation in their care. The Department also has a major responsibility for American Indian reservation communities and for people who live in island territories under U.S. administration.

The Minerals Management Service Mission

As a bureau of the Department of the Interior, the Minerals Management Service's (MMS) primary responsibilities are to manage the mineral resources located on the Nation's Outer Continental Shelf (OCS), collect revenue from the Federal OCS and onshore Federal and Indian lands, and distribute those revenues.

Moreover, in working to meet its responsibilities, the **Offshore Minerals Management Program** administers the OCS competitive leasing program and oversees the safe and environmentally sound exploration and production of our Nation's offshore natural gas, oil and other mineral resources. The MMS **Minerals Revenue Management** meets its responsibilities by ensuring the efficient, timely and accurate collection and disbursement of revenue from mineral leasing and production due to Indian tribes and allottees, States and the U.S. Treasury.

The MMS strives to fulfill its responsibilities through the general guiding principles of: (1) being responsive to the public's concerns and interests by maintaining a dialogue with all potentially affected parties and (2) carrying out its programs with an emphasis on working to enhance the quality of life for all Americans by lending MMS assistance and expertise to economic development and environmental protection.